From Grief to Joy (The Second Year is Harder)

An Interactive Workbook for Healing the Heart

Written by Suzanne Wachtel, LCSW

About the Author

Suzanne Wachtel, LCSW is a seasoned, licensed clinical social worker who is a no-nonsense life coach, psychotherapist and healer.

She arms us with a bag of tools to help us heal and recover from the deep wounds of loss.

Suzanne has loved and lost as many of us have and through her positive strategies and her kindness has helped many recover and heal. Suzanne has been in private practice for 15 years both in New York and Boca Raton, Florida. She runs workshops on grief nationwide to help others Recover and find the answers and closure they need to move on.

My Favorite Quote:
If I should ever leave you whom I love
To go along the silten way. Grieve not.
Nor speak of me with tears.
But laugh and talk of me as if I were beside you
there.
And when you hear a song or see a bird I
loved.
Please do not let the thought of me be sad.
For I am loving you just as I always have…
There are so many things I wanted still to do…
So many things to say to you…
Remenber that I did not fear…
It was just leaving you that was so hard to face
We cannot see beyond…
But this I know:
I loved you so- 'twas heaven here with you
Eternal rest grant unto him, O lord, and let
Perpetual light shin upon him.

CONTENTS

Healing

"One of the best ways to make myself happy is to make other people happy;

One of the best way to make other people happy is… to be happy myself."

Introduction

My name is Suzanne Wachtel and I'm a licensed clinical social worker. I have a private practice in Boca Raton, Florida and I host a variety of workshops nationally and internationally.

Recently, I have been asked to do workshops on grief. I can truly say that yes, I have become a "grief expert." Between November 2013 and February 2014 I lost my mother in a painful, dragged out death, put down my 14-year-old golden lab, and that week my son accidentally overdosed and died using heroin. So I guess I have become a true expert on loss and grief.

My workshop on grief is uplifting, inspiring and healing. Learning to process loss and the feelings that come with it can be challenging. Learning skills and tools that take away the darkness of death can be liberating.

Chapter One

Manifestation of Grief

Grieving the death of a loved one is very painful and at times can be overwhelming. Individuals often worry if they are grieving "the right way" and question if they are "normal." Grief is not just sadness or depression; it's a whole host of feelings and emotions. Besides affecting your emotions, grief reaches into every part of your life: your work, your relationships with others and your image of yourself. Not everyone will have the same experiences.

1. profound feeling of sadness, emptiness and loss of meaning
2. a feeling of tightness in your chest, your throat or your abdomen
3. an empty feeling in the stomach
4. the need to sigh
5. muscle weakness
6. stomach aches, head aches
7. weight loss or gain
8. an extreme weakness and lack of energy
9. the need to go through a detailed review of all the events that lead to the death
10. an intense preoccupation with the life and memories of the deceased; and the need to re-examine past actions and behavior toward your loved one
11. occasional feelings of regrets over things that happened or didn't happen in your relationship with the deceased
12. the urge to try and solve the puzzle which led to the death; attempting to make some sense out of the course of illness
13. the inability to concentrate; you may be absent-minded (get lost while driving; misplace money; miss appointments)
14. loneliness
15. you may be sensitive to noise

16. may have difficulty sleeping
17. you may dream frequently about the deceased (or wish you did)
18. occasional untypical anger (at the doctor, G-d, or the deceased for leaving you)
19. a feeling of numbness
20. a sense that nothing seems real to you
21. you may start or increase your smoking or drinking habits
22. you may have uncontrolled tears
23. you can become restless and engage in aimless activity
24. at times you try to avoid any reminder of the deceased, or you may become fascinated with objects, activities or places associated with your loved one
25. you may withdraw or avoid seeing friends or family
26. you may hear or see your loved one—sensing their presence like expecting the person to arrive home at the usual time, hearing their voice or seeing their face
27. sometimes you fear you will forget what the person looked like or you will forget the good memories
28. you may take comfort in wearing treasured belongings or treasured articles from the deceased

Chapter Two

Please Understand

My_____died.

There—it's down in black and white. What I mean is, they are still alive in spirit, but their body died. And that's how I became a member of the community of the bereaved, and as a member, I ask for your understanding.

As individuals, we in the community of the bereaved need you. Don't worry about saying the right things. We're tired of clichés. We know our "dear ones are at peace with God" and they feel no more pain.

But we still miss their physical presence. There was this one person on earth to whom we were the most important, one person who knew us so completely that no words were necessary. We miss that.

If we seem distant, please understand. Some of us are still in shock. If we seem angry, please understand. Most of us are angry, but we know that God accepts our anger and refines it into an energy that will be vital in our outreach to others.

If tears come at inappropriate times and places, please understand. Our emotions, even yet, are still raw. Just when we think we are in control, a song or a scent—or a feeling of utter desolation—overcomes us.

Or, if we laugh, know that deep inside we are hurting. We know that God has given us the gift of a sense of humor, and that our loved ones are rejoicing that we are exercising this gift.

We may be forgetful, sleep is elusive; we may not eat properly; we may make foolish purchases. Please don't condemn us. Just know it can be a part of the grieving process. In time, we'll come around

And please, oh please, let us follow our own timetables. We each march or stumble along the route at our own pace. Grief has no calendar; don't hold us to a timetable. For the moment, we are drifting, buoyed by the love of our family, friends and faith. This faith, along with your understanding, will enable us—eventually—to celebrate life once again.

So please be patient, include us, excuse us, invite us and understand that we are healing and in our own time we will be OK.

Chapter Three

Death

Death is permanent. It is truly the only thing that cannot be changed. The only thing we can do about death is to learn the tools to deal with the loss and to teach others how to understand.

Death is the topic most people have trouble talking about. It's almost as if talking about it will bring it close to them. We need to start speaking about death, understanding it and forming ways to cope and process. When death touches our lives and people or pets that are special to us die, we need the tools to heal and grieve.

Many cultures have a variety of beliefs that are comforting and embrace community and spirituality. Our brains struggle to make sense of death, as we cannot understand what we cannot feel, touch or see.

Q.) What is your interpretation of death?

A). _____

Chapter Four

Death Rituals

There are a large variety of rituals and traditions surrounding the death passage. From funerals to eulogies, to shivas, cremating, burials and scattering ashes, the end of the physical life is held with great importance and honor.

From Catholic to Jewish, Hindu, Christian or Buddhist, all religions and philosophies use rituals and traditions to mark the passing and ending of a life.

When that is all said and done, the numbness wears off, the people go home and now the process of grief within us truly begins.

How do you wrap your head around losing someone who can't be replaced? It's hard to understand something so permanent which we know so little about: This workshop is designed to explore and heal.

Chapter Five

<u>Spirituality</u>

What hurts more?

Losing a parent?

Losing a spouse?

Losing a friend?

Losing a partner?

Losing a child?

Losing a grandchild?

Losing a pet?

Loss is loss. Pain is pain. Devastation is not able to be described! There is no way to measure loss and pain. It is personal, individual and experienced by everyone in their own way. Acceptance is key…it hurts.

Chapter Six

Grief

Q). How does your family grieve?

A).

_____

_____

_____

_____

Q). What rituals were you brought up with surrounding death?

A).

_____

_____

_____

_____

Q). When did you first experience death?

A).

_____

_____

_____

_____

The pain you feel when someone dies never leaves you but…suffering is a choice!

Chapter Seven

<u>Joy</u>

Joy is the goal of this process. Your life will never be the same but it can be better if you let it. Suffering is a choice.

Taking care of yourself, continuing to keep your loved ones in your memories and life, celebrating their birthdays, finding the bird or butterfly or song that you know is for you from them. These bring me joy.

What takes you from grief to joy?

_____
_____
_____
_____

Q). Will this pain last forever?

A). No, it will not last forever, but you will be changed forever.

You deserve to have a happy heart!

Chapter Eight

What Brings Peace?

The first year when my mother, dog Sammy and son Adam died within eight weeks of each other, I thought my life would never be normal again. This amount of loss was crazy. I went into survival mode using every tool in my book! Moved to Florida, pulled the rest of the family together and started over.

That first year I felt like a true survivor—an absolute warrior. I helped everyone else and only had a few painful pitfalls but I was determined not to let these losses define my life. I learned how to really find the positive and in this process I discovered a true buried treasure:

The meaning and value of the life we do have!

Smile when you see a sign that reminds you of your

loved ones (a coin bird, butterfly, etc).

Chapter Nine

Year One

Every day year one, I felt strong and enlightened. I figured out that the gift of life is only temporary and can be taken away at any moment each day.

So, I made a strong decision to live richer, choose healthy, like-minded people and always look for the lesson and the silver lining in every situation.

Then came year two: I imagined it would be easier, but I was wrong. Year two means that this is not a temporary situation, it means that these people are permanently removed from our world! It's scary to think I may forget them, their laugh, smell or voice. More than ever I work harder getting to know them and memorize more details.

"People are truly gone when they are

forgotten."

Chapter Ten

First Year Questions

Q). How did you feel during the first year after the death?

A).

_____

_____

_____

_____

Q). What did you do to help the grief?
A)._____

_____

_____

_____

Q). What was different year two? Did memories fade? Was it more or less painful?
A)._____

_____

_____

_____

Find the way from grief to joy!

Chapter Eleven

What Brings you Hope?

Make a list:
- friends
- meditating
- going to the grave
- talking about the person who is gone
- looking for signs: birds, flowers, butterflies
- yoga, breathing
- nature
- looking at photos, remembering the joy they brought to me life
- knowing that they are still with me as guardian angels and feeling my son, dog and mom's energy around me every day.

Q). What do you see or feel?
List:
1._____

_____

2._____

_____

3._____

_____

The love in your heart never fades—ever.

Chapter Twelve

Forever

"I'll never see him/ her again"

Respond:

"I'll never feel them again, hug them or hear their voice"

Respond:

"Recreating a favorite meal, cooking a favorite dish. When I cook my

mom's favorite recipe for mac and cheese, the house smells like she's still

alive and cooking in my house. I almost expect her to be sitting there. It also

taste so good.

Respond:

Doing something you enjoyed when they were alive like going to a movie,

making cookies, taking a walk, etc. Do them!

Respond:

Mediums can answer your questions…

Chapter Thirteen

Mediums?

Do they help? Mediums (if authentic) can help a great deal. They believe that energy is the life in our bodies, our souls. Some people have a gift of being able to hear, see and feel what most of us cannot. Mediums bring a spiritual component to the mystery of the afterlife, of the energy living on after the body has died.

In my personal experience, mediums knew details that proved to me that what they were saying was impossible to make up. The mediums I went to helped me understand, process and heal. Knowing my loved ones were safe, content and with me all of the time. It was comforting at a time when pain and hurt were on my mind and nothing made sense. However, I found great clarity and closure speaking with a medium when I felt lost. It helped me and many others.

If someone is connected to you with love they become your guardian angel and are with you forever (in my opinion).

Chapter Fourteen

Questions About Mediums

Q). What is your belief about speaking to a medium?

A).

_____

_____

_____

_____

Q). Did it bring clarity, closure or understanding to the death?

A).

_____

_____

_____

_____

Q). What did you gain from the experience? Good or bad

A).

_____

_____

_____

_____

Q). Would you suggest others seek comfort from a medium?

A).

_____

_____

_____

_____

Signs to look for:
Pennies from heaven (coins)
Butterflies
Sunsets
Clouds
Birds
Rainbows

Chapter Fifteen

<u>Signs from Heaven</u>

This is my favorite part!

I've been seeing signs from the universe since my grandma died. I felt that her love and our bond was so pure and heartfelt that I know she never left me. For years I saw her in a red-breasted robin every spring. I also smelled her at times in the house and twice I dreamed that she came to the house at night and I let her hold my children both five and two years old. She kissed their heads and held me in her arms. It was so real.

I see birds for all my loved ones; My mom is a wild parrot, my son Adam is a dove, Helen is a blue jay, and Carole a red cardinal. The birds visit me and I sense the connection.

Dreams are true visits when we are blessed to

receive one. Rejoice!

Chapter Sixteen

Signs

A. Make a list of your loved ones who you have lost (Pets, too):

1.

_____

2.

_____

3.

_____

4.

_____

5.

_____

B. Make a list of any signs that you have felt from them, e.g. coins, birds, flowers, coincidences, look-alikes.

_____
_____
_____
_____

C. How do you feel when you hear that song or notice the coins?
Response:

_____
_____
_____
_____

Celebrate Life!

Not the one moment of death

"Healing Your Heart"
Meditation is very healing
Go to:
www.rockmyyoga.com

Jeana Lynn has spent 20 years focused on her passion for healthy mind and body connection. Jeana, author of "Bliss," a self-help guide to inner peace, has combined her studies to produce Rock Om Yoga and meditations. Her meditations are unique and a very powerful tool for transformation and healing. Jeana believes that along with changing our thoughts, we need to move and heal our energy through meditation and crystals.

Download: "Healing Your Heart" meditation written and narrated by Jeana Lynn, an expert on healing through energy and crystals.

Therapy and counseling are support systems

and comfort that are priceless.

Chapter Seventeen

Therapy

Therapy – Grief Counseling – Bereavement

Does it help?

What is it?

This is a time in life when therapy can be extremely helpful. It's an opportunity to work through the pain, pick it apart, go through the stages allowing yourself to heal with someone to help you.

To suffer in silence is not the answer. Groups that have bereavement can be very helpful and being with a group of people that truly know what you are feeling can be priceless.

Most areas have hospice, temples, churches or other private sectors that host bereavement groups. Often they meet once a week and can comfort along with introduce you to other like-minded people. Give it a try. Some people swear by it. I do.

Chapter Eighteen

The Memories Never Die

People are only truly gone…when they are forgotten!

Think about them, talk about them, make them part of your daily routine.

A). List special memories:
1. _____
2. _____
3. _____

Ask them questions, tell them what you are doing and if you are quiet

enough and just listen, you will get your answer.

B). Write down any times you have tried this:

1. _____
2. _____
3. _____
4. _____
5. _____

Death is a natural cycle in each life, embrace it.

Chapter Nineteen

Some Things That Help

- Celebrating Birthdays

- Memories

- Keep out Photographs

- Tell Stories (good and bad)

- Visit the Grave if That Comforts You

- Go to Nature to Find Comfort—Beach, Woods, Water

- Go to Yoga to Find Peace

- Hug a Tree, Nothing Better than Hugging a Beautiful Tree and Feel the Energy Hugging You Back. I Pretend It's My Son...Feels Good.

There are no rules in grief, only strategies to help the healing.

A Word From the Author

I hope that this workbook and its exercises will help heal your wounds, even if ever so slightly. There is no easy way to get through loss, no way to skip over the hard stuff.

Just know that everyone grieves in his or her own way, we heal at our own pace and know that it's OK—you are not alone.

This book was designed to teach strategies and give tools to people suffering the pain of loss.

I was not an expert and had no idea how much it hurt and how lonely and empty it felt until it happened to me.

I can't promise that you will snap out of it, but I can say with confidence that working through it makes the process easier.

Healing Is Really Important! The only way to take you from grief to joy!

<u>Contact Information</u>

Suzanne Wachtel, LCSW is available

for lectures, workshops and private

one-on-one coaching therapy sessions.

Website: www.therapy-boca.com

Facebook: SuzanneWachtelLCSW

Email: swachtelcsw@gmail.com

Telephone: 631-525-3646

Notes

Notes

Notes

Notes

Notes

Notes